M000194045

Ladynomics

Ladynomics

A Woman's Prescription
for Wealth and Financial Well-Being

Randi B. Nelson, MD, MBA

LADYNOMICS

Published by Purposely Created Publishing Group™

Copyright © 2019 Randi Nelson

All rights reserved.

No part of this book may be reproduced, distributed or transmitted in any form by any means, graphic, electronic, or mechanical, including photocopy, recording, taping, or by any information storage or retrieval system, without permission in writing from the publisher, except in the case of reprints in the context of reviews, quotes, or references.

Printed in the United States of America

ISBN: 978-1-949134-88-9

Special discounts are available on bulk quantity purchases by book clubs, associations and special interest groups. For details email: sales@publishyourgift.com or call (888) 949-6228.

For information logon to:
www.PublishYourGift.com

DEDICATION

I dedicate this book to my family, especially my mother Cislyn, my brother Michael, my niece Layla and my father Rainford, who rests in heaven. I also dedicate to all the people who complete my circle, including Samaad, all my extended family, and my close circles of sister and brother friends.

I love and appreciate you all.

Dr. Randi

TABLE OF CONTENTS

INTRODUCTION

I've lived a fairly successful life. I graduated from high school, college (getting early admission to the accounting program SUNY Buffalo), and graduate (MBA) and medical school. In medical school, I won the Gold Humanism Honor Society and was the medical school Class of 2009 awardee for the Most Likely to Bring the Class Together Award. I received many awards ever since I was in elementary school; in ninth grade, I received so many awards they called me Michael Jackson, because at that time, he had won eight Grammys. I got my first job with Morgan Stanley, the world-renowned investment bank, right out of undergraduate, and was promoted to Vice President at Citigroup. At age 29, I purchased my own home, where I would entertain friends on a regular basis. In 2005, I was accepted to medical school. I finally found real love at age 46 on Election Night 2016 at the Jacob Javits Center.

However, there were some valleys through which I travelled, which included the separation of my parents (which suddenly thrusted my mother into the head of household role) when I was young, bad relationships, September 11th (which occurred three blocks from my place of employment), and the death of my father in 2000. He was my biggest cheerleader; although my father was disabled and sustained himself on a monthly $900 disability check, he would always purchase a salmon filet for me because he knew I loved it. The culmination of these events would lead me to undergo some significant changes in my life.

I have always strived to ascend to the next level in my personal life and professional life. Being an investment banking accountant for several years, I thought I was doing okay. However, after witnessing the destruction on September 11th, 2001, and most importantly after losing my father, I knew that I had to do more with my talents than crunching numbers for large financial organizations. Those events were the impetus for me to leave investment banking and become a physician.

One of the major reasons for my decision was my desire to do more for the people I love, especially my family and friends. There is nothing I enjoy more than to contribute to their comfort. I am also community driven; I would love to do more in terms of charity. The more prosperous I am, the more that I can give to those less fortunate. My father was disabled, and I know first-hand the importance of charity and compassion to those who are not as fortunate and blessed as I have been in my life.

My desire is to assist others to become financially secure so that they can live their lives as they wish.

CHAPTER 1

Why Do We Need Financial Wellness?

An investment in knowledge pays the best interest.

—**Benjamin Franklin**

Why do we need financial wellness? What is financial wellness? The definition of financial wellness varies depending on who you ask. However, this definition offered by Robert Powell, a contributor to *USA Today*, encompasses what I think it means the most: "Financial wellness is a state of financial well-being where you have: minimal financial stress; a strong financial foundation (little or no debt, an emergency savings fund, and are living below your means); and a plan you are following that puts you on track to meet future financial goals."

It means you are undertaking the process of managing your finances efficiently and successfully.

Why is it important? Just take a look at these statistics:

According to Student Loan Hero (Studentloanhero. com), Americans are inundated with debt. Americans hold over $1 trillion dollars in credit card debt, with the average credit cardholder holding a balance of over $5,000 dollars. Americans have $15 trillion in mortgage debt and $1.1 trillion in auto loan debt. Over 43 million people hold medical debt with a balance of nearly $1,800. With this level of debt, it is no wonder that Americans are having a difficult time making ends meet. Many are finding it difficult to pay their everyday expenses.

According to a recent report from Career Builders, 75 percent of full-time workers are living paycheck to paycheck, and having a high salary does not shield you from this reality. The study notes that individuals making over $100,000 also admit to living paycheck to paycheck. Nearly 70 percent of American workers are in debt, and many of them feel that their debt is unmanageable. As a result of this level of debt, savings and investments are suffering. According to this survey, the average American has less than $5,000 in savings, and the average retirement account for those aged 55 to 64 is just $120,000.

This is a meager amount, and most retirees with this amount of savings or less will outlive their savings.

Who should care about financial wellness? Well, everyone. It is for the young and mature in age. It does not matter if you are initiating your first financial transaction—whether that be opening up a checking account or savings account or receiving your first paycheck—or if you are in your sixties and finalizing your retirement plans. It is never too early to think about financial wellness. If you are in your late teens or early twenties, are college bound, and think you have to take out loans, you have to be concerned about financial wellness. If you are in your late twenties or thirties, have started a new job, are looking to purchase property and establish financial accounts, including opening up those first credit cards, you have to be concerned about financial wellness. Once you enter your forties and fifties, you become concerned with retirement and financing in those later years in life. And in your sixties and seventies, you're concerned about sufficiency and having enough money to satisfy your financial needs.

You may be wondering why a physician would care about financial wellness. Many do not realize that financial security is intrinsically tied to health, as individuals who are steeped in worry regarding their finances may begin to note changes in their health and overall well-being. Stress weakens the immune system, which makes us more vulnerable to infection and disease. Stress makes us more susceptible to the common cold, flu, chronic disease, food allergies, high blood pressure, heart disease, and digestive problems. Those suffering from chronic stress may experience anxiety, depression, and sleep problems. This stress can also disrupt the family unit and relationships. Lack of financial wellness is responsible for distress in relationships and marriages. One of the main causes of divorce is issues with money. We desire to have enough money to take care of our family and meet our everyday needs. In addition, we want to secure our future and the future of our children and perhaps of our parents. Lack of financial wellness and security disrupts peace of mind.

As a former investment banking accountant, I understand the importance of financial knowledge and literacy. As a physician, my task is to help maintain the health of my patients. Empowering individuals in financial literacy and knowledge results in greater health and well-being in families.

NOTES

NOTES

NOTES

NOTES

CHAPTER 2

Mindset

Once your mindset changes, everything on the outside will change along with it.

—Steve Maraboli

Why is mindset important? You cannot get on the right track with negative thinking. You have to get rid of negative thinking in order to make and attract opportunities that will assist you on your path to financial wellness. Ask yourself the following questions: Are you aware of your own negative thinking patterns? Generally speaking, what is your mindset at this point in your life? What do you think or say about money? Do you believe that money is the root of all evil? Or that rich people are all evil? If you feel that money is the root of all evil, it is going be very difficult to use money to get you on the right track. Growing up in your household, what was the discussion around money? Everyone had a different experience. Some people had healthy discussions regarding finance. Some people had no discussion regarding finance. Many families feel that it isn't right to focus on money only. In my family, we really didn't discuss money. We didn't talk about investing. My father was disabled, so his monthly check covered his basic needs, such as food, clothing, and shelter. My mother was the primary breadwinner. As a data entry clerk, her salary covered the basics. There really wasn't much left for luxuries such as dining out, movie outings, or extracurricular activities. Although she invested in her 401(k), we never had discussions about stocks and bonds and the importance of setting aside money for the future. I am unsure whether my mother understood the intricacies of the market. We really were trying to make ends meet. Amazingly, my mother's salary covered all of our needs, though not necessarily our wants.

Think about the people with whom you hang around. What messages are you directly or indirectly receiving from them? How do they influence you? Are you hanging around people who discuss investing and saving for the future? Or do you hang around with people who are always saying that they are broke? Are they using their money to buy the latest designer gear? Are they living paycheck to paycheck or on credit without any thought to investing and saving for the future or becoming debt free?

I used to hold the mentality that all I ever need is enough to cover my expenses and some basic saving and investment goals. The idea of abundance and having more than enough was never in my thought process. Until recently.

What do you have to do to get the right mindset? Well, wishful thinking is not enough. You have to put words into action. There are a number of ways to change your thought process. The number-one thing to do is forgive yourself. Forgive yourself for mistakes you made in the past regarding your finances. Forgive your family for however they may have contributed to your current financial state. Britney Castro, a financial advisor, stated, "Forgiveness is a powerful tool because it prevents us from being a prisoner to our past. If we shift our focus away from shame, we can make room for better practices and a healthier attitude towards money." It's important to acknowledge and accept what has happened. Make apologies to yourself (and those around you, where necessary) and focus on moving forward.

Another tip is to start reading books on wealth and money management. When I first started working in the investment banking industry many moons ago, I used to read a great deal on investing because I desired a greater understanding of money management and the various investment financial products. I wanted to gain a better understanding of wealth and not to be intimidated by it.

Another tool is affirmations. Affirmations can help you change your negative thinking patterns. You can actually make up your own affirmations or read books that provide affirmations for you. Examples of affirmations include "I am wealthy," "I am debt free," "I will have X amount of dollars in my retirement account," and "I will have X amount of dollars for my children's education."

Relatedly, visualization is a powerful tool. I love doing this and consider myself an expert at it. I imagine the life that I want. I then start making decisions that attract opportunities that move me towards my goal. That's why vision boards are so popular these days. It is a tool to assist you in changing your thoughts and to help you see what you want for the future. For example, in May of 2017, I decided to submit an article or story for the *Chicken Soup for the Soul* series. I believed that my story would be featured in the book, and it was. My journey to becoming a doctor was the same. Once I made up my mind, I took the necessary step towards my goal.

Fourteen years after deciding I would be a physician, my dream became a reality.

The last tool and probably the most important is to always show gratitude. Always be thankful for what you have.

NOTES

NOTES

NOTES

NOTES

NOTES

CHAPTER 3

Abundance in Thought and Deed

Abundance is not something we acquire. It is something we tune into.

—Wayne Dyer

What is abundance? It simply means ample quantity of an item. Many of us think of abundance in terms of wealth and money. However, abundance can pertain to love, peace of mind, and freedom. How to obtain it remains the same in all instances. I spent a lot of time talking about mindset because it is very important in having a consciousness of abundance.

How do we obtain abundance? We don't. We tap into it because it's all around us. Really, it's just the matter of being aware and conscious of it and knowing that we are in it and that we have it at any time in our lives. It is that simple. But it's really a hard concept to grasp because there's so much negativity around us. There is so much focus on lack—lack of money, lack of love, and lack of peace. We are surrounded by messages that we have to do whatever is necessary to get what we need, even if that calls for unethical means, when in fact, it's right there for us to grab.

So what blocks our path to abundance? And how do we get rid of it? The main block is our thinking, primarily negative thinking. How do we get rid of negative thinking? Here are a couple of tips. You truly have to believe you deserve abundance and that you can have financial well-being. That's just it. Creating an abundance consciousness is very similar to setting up the correct mindset. Again, affirmations and visualization are wonderful tools. The key is to be committed to change in your thought process. If negative thoughts creep in, immediately think of something different. Think of where you'd like to be in five to fifteen years. Remember you are here today because of your thoughts and actions. It's the law of attraction. You basically attract what you are and what you think about. The beautiful thing is once you shift your thought process, things will begin to change, and you'll begin a path of health and peace. Again, this doesn't only pertain to money. You can use this with relationships. For example, if you don't believe you are worthy of someone good and wonderful, most likely you will not meet someone who possess those attributes.

The second tip to tuning into abundance is giving. This doesn't necessarily mean giving money. You can give your time, your talent, or just your attention to someone in need. It's good karma. Basically, what you give comes back to you. And some believe that what comes to you comes back tenfold. However, the purpose of giving is not just to get something in return. You do it because it's the right thing to do.

Be clear about what you want and how you want to achieve it. Claim it. Remember abundance surrounds you all the time. All you have to do is tune into it. The end result will be more opportunities. You will meet individuals who are on the same wavelength as you are and who will help you achieve the goals you have set out for yourself in the realm of financial wellness. It's really a win-win situation. But the key is to believe it and understand that abundance is yours for the taking.

NOTES

NOTES

NOTES

NOTES

NOTES

CHAPTER 4

Getting Started

The journey of a thousand miles begins with one step.

—Lao Tzu

Right after you decide you are going to get on the right path towards financial wellness and independence, you have to get an honest assessment of where you stand now. The first step is to gather *all* of your financial records. This includes the following: credit card statements, student loan statements, banking and investment statements, several months of utility bills, mortgage of rental statements, car notes, day care or school expenses, home or rental insurance, car insurance, and groceries. If you need help gathering all your expenses, inspect your bank and/or credit card statements to get an idea of what you spend each month. Many credit card online programs provide summaries of your charges for a period of time. Financial companies such as American Express and Bank of America will even categorize your expenses, which will further assist you in your budgeting.

The next step will be organizing your information. I prefer paperless, but some statements are still mailed to me. So I purchase one of those accordion folders from Staples (or any home office store) and begin to categorize and file appropriately. You can also file information in an online folder. There are many online programs, such as Quick Books, Mint, and Evernote, that help with organization. I am old school (and a former accountant), so I file and have my information close to me. Again, this will assist you with organization and provide you with a good handle of where you stand now.

After compiling your paperwork (or online folders), categorize and separate your expenses between fixed expenses and variable expenses. A fixed expense is an expense you incur on a regular basis, and the expense amount is the essentially the same each period. Examples of fixed expenses would be your monthly mortgage or rental payment, your car note, and day care or babysitting fees. These figures usually remain the same throughout the year unless there is an increase in your rent or changes to your taxes that will affect your mortgage payment. Some fixed expenses can be quarterly depending on how you choose to make your payments. For example my disability and life insurance are quarterly. List all of the expenses regardless of whether you pay monthly or quarterly. Later on, we will discuss how to account for these non-monthly expenses. Next, you will want to list your variable expenses. This is where it gets a bit difficult, because variable expenses are not necessarily the same each month, and they could take up a good portion of your monthly spending. A good example is grocery expenses. You may budget about $500 per month, but your spending may vary depending on extenuating circumstances. So one month it may be $500, but it may be $700 the following month because you had visitors to whom you provided meals. Retrieve your previous statements and all your groceries and dining-out expenses for a full 12 months and then divide by 12. That should give you an idea of how much you should attribute to your monthly grocery and dining out expenses per month. Here is an example of Karen's grocery expense calculation. She would like to spend $500 per month. However, she should budget $550 per month because she has some months where she spends a little bit more, especially during the summer months and holiday season.

KAREN'S GROCERIES EXPENSE CALCULATION		
Actual Expenses:		
January		(500)
February		(500)
March		(500)
April		(500)
May		(500)
June		(700)
July		(600)
August		(500)
September		(500)
October		(500)
November		(500)
December		(800)
	Subtotal	(6,600)
	Divided by 12	(550)
	Grocery Budget amount	**$ (550)**

Another variable expense would be entertainment. Depending on the season or happenings in your life, you may spend more during one period of time versus another. For example, I find that I spend more money on entertainment during the summer than I would in the winter because there are more activities I enjoy in the summer, such as outdoor concerts and summer festivals, than there are in the winter. The opposite may occur for you. If you are an avid skier or into winter sports and activities, you will find that your expenses are higher in the winter or fall months. The basic idea is to get an understanding of what was spent during the past year so that you can apply an average amount to your monthly budget. This will be crucial because once your budget and your goals are set, you will be able to make changes that will assist you in achieving them. Honestly, you may even be surprised at how much money you spend on variable items. Sometimes these items are what cause your budget to run amok. You know how you go to the bank or ATM and take out of $50, and by the end of the week or maybe even the end of the day, you have no idea where that money went? The money most likely went to those miscellaneous expenses such as a cup of coffee or tea or pastries. It is these items that will screw up a budget. One thing that I find very useful is to keep a small notebook or use the notes application on your smartphone and track every single dollar that you spent. Doing so will give you an idea of those "ghost" expenses that you may not even be aware of. You are aware of your mortgage or rent expenses. But it's these miscellaneous expenses that makes budgeting difficult—and what make it necessary. It's very similar to the tracking system in weight management. You literally input everything that you've consumed for the day. I have participated in the Weight Watchers Points system, and I am amazed at all the "ghost" food that I take in a day. My fixed meals would be breakfast, lunch, and dinner. But then all my "ghost" intake would be those items like the pretzel or that one cookie that we take no notice of. But it's those miscellaneous items that will throw off our diet. It works the same way with managing money. It is necessary to have a strict accounting of our expenditures of the money we bring in.

NOTES

NOTES

NOTES

NOTES

CHAPTER 5

Goal Setting, Budgeting, and Figuring Out Where You Stand Now (Your Net Worth)

The goal isn't more money.
The goal is living life on your terms.

—**Will Rogers**

Once you have everything that you'll need for your budget, the next step is setting goals. What is it that you want to accomplish with your money? Where do you see yourself in one year? Five years? How much money would you like in retirement? If you are renting a home now, when do you want to purchase a home? And how much do you think you'd like to spend? Again, the best thing to do is write these goals and make them concrete. If you are married or in a relationship, this is something you would discuss with your partner. If you have children, what would you like to save for college? Goals can be categorized by short-term goals versus long-term goals. A short-term goal would be a goal that you want to accomplish within a year or two. That could be the money that you need to save for a vacation, home improvement, furniture, or your emergency fund. A long-term goal is a goal you'd like to accomplish more than two years into your future or throughout your life. That can include savings for a home, retirement, or a car. The beauty about goal setting is it helps guard against impulsive spending. If you know you have a goal that you'd like to obtain, the likelihood that you will carelessly spend money should or will go down. For example, if you decide that your goal is to attend college, you have to prioritize your spending so that you are able to save more. When I decided I wanted to go to medical school, the first thing I eliminated was acrylic nails. I love polished nails, but I had to make a choice at that time because I wanted to accumulate as much money as I could since

I was unable to work during medical school. It was an easy choice for me. Similarly, if you know you want to buy a car with all cash up front, you may need to think twice about spending money on a very expensive clothing item or accessories that you may not need at the very moment. Taking time to think about what you really want will assist you in prioritizing your financial goals.

The next step would be to prioritize your goals, meaning deciding what you feel is important to achieve first. Normally, you would want to achieve your short-term goals first. The next step would be to conquer your long-term goals. Each decision is definitely a personal one. This is when the advice of a financial advisor may come in handy. After medical school, I decided to take the approach of paying off debt, increasing my investment, and saving for retirement simultaneously. I've taken this approach because retirement is within a 20-year period for me. So yes, it is considered long term, but I do not want to forgo the opportunity to make money on the money that time allows. I also want to take advantage of money that my employer will match. At this point in my life, if I waited until all my debts were paid, including school loans, I may miss the opportunity to take advantage of time that would allow my retirement savings to grow and my employer 401(k) contributions, which are considered "free money." If you are young person and you for some reason you find yourself in a great deal of debt, perhaps it would make more sense to pay off debts first, then start saving for an emergency fund, then move on to investing, including investing for retirement. These are decisions you should work out with a trusted financial advisor. In any situation, place your goals on paper (or on your computer). What are all your goals? Once you have figured that out, go ahead and categorize them, dividing goals into short term and long term, and prioritize them. This is an exercise you should do no matter your age.

NET WORTH

What is net worth? Net worth is a valuable statement that calculates your assets (or items you own) vs. your liabilities (items you owe). Your total assets are your property or tangible items that you own, such as artwork, your car, jewelry, stocks, bonds, investments, and cash you have on hand. Liabilities are items you owe, such as credit card debt, personal loans, and car loans.

How do you calculate it? Tally up the value of all of your assets and all your liabilities. You will need a realistic valuation of your property, which may be a bit difficult because the value is subjective and may vary depending on the person who is assessing the value. One source may say that your home is worth $300K, and another may say it is worth $250K. For your home assessment, you may have to seek the assistance of a home inspector or home assessor. You could also look at value of recent sales of the homes in the neighborhood to get an idea of your home's worth. There are online research sources that you can utilize. For example, Chase Bank and RE/MAX have online home worth assessments. If you own a car, you can use online resources such as Kelley Blue Book to get your car assessed or valued. Cash and investments are a bit easier. All you have to do is look at your current statements to get an idea of your stocks, bonds, mutual funds, checking account, and savings account. Those figures are absolute. To calculate your net worth, subtract the total of your liabilities from the total of your assets.

Why is having a net worth statement important? Because it gives you real-time information regarding your financial worth at a particular point in time. It also provides a snapshot of your financial health and solvency that will be valuable to third parties, such as a bank. Your goal is to always have your assets greater than your liability. A third party like a bank may look at your net worth statements when they make their decision regarding mortgage or car loan. If you find yourself in a situation where your liabilities are greater than your assets, you should work to reverse the situation.

Here is a sample net worth statement.

SAMPLE NET WORTH STATEMENT			
Assets		**Liabilities**	
Home Value	$ 300,000	Mortgage	$ 174,000
Cash	$ 25,000	Student Loans	$ 200,000
Car	$ 15,000	Car Loan	$ 5,000
401(k)	$ 100,000	Credit Cards	$ 15,000
Vanguard	$ 25,000		
Art	$ 15,000		
Other Personal Property	$ 10,000		
Total Assets	$ 490,000	**Total Liabilities**	$ 394,000
		Net Worth	$ 96,000
		(Total Assets - Total Liabilities)	

DEBT REDUCTION

In my net worth example above, this person's net worth statement is positive because their assets are greater than their liabilities. But suppose the opposite was true, meaning their net worth was negative? For example, once medical students graduate from medical school, they will often find that their net worth is negative, most likely due to school loans, which average approximately $200,000.

How do we reduce debt? Here are a number of strategies that may be utilized:

- ❯ Pay off high-interest-rate loans or liabilities first. If you have credit card debt at a 20 percent interest rate and have a private loan at a 10 percent interest rate, pay off that 20 percent debt first.

- ❯ Once you pay off a balance, apply the extra money towards a different credit card or loan balance. For example, for the past two years, you have been paying $200 towards a credit card balance of $1,800. Now that that balance is paid off, use the $200 and apply it towards another loan or credit card.

- ❯ Renegotiate interest rates if you carry balances at high interest rates.

❯ Always pay more than the minimum payment on a credit card or loan balance.

❯ If you receive a bonus or any sort of lump sum of money, instead of spending it, apply it towards credit cards or loan balances.

❯ If you have debt, do not add to your total balance by applying for more debt. Pay off what you currently hold.

❯ Find a second source of income (e.g. a second job) or increase income or reduce expenses and apply money saved or earned to liabilities.

BUDGETING

A budget is a statement of expected expenditures and income. Basically, it's a plan or forecast that states your income for a certain period of time versus the expenses you anticipate having to pay. A budget is extremely important because it provides the blueprint for how you spend and save your money. It also tells you if you if there is anything to save at the end of the period. Most budgets are monthly. Most people are paid once or usually twice a month if they are employed. If they are self-employed, their income may be more variable. But the key is to estimate your income as accurately as possible and list all of your expenses so that you have the most accurate view of your cash flow each month.

So what are the steps for putting a budget together? Let's take a look.

In Chapter 4, I spoke about gathering all of your financial information, including credit card statements, student loan statements, car loan statements, stocks and bonds statements, investment account statements, and bank statements.

To start your budget, you want to list your income, which is what you bring in or anticipate bringing in each month. Then you will start listing the expenses you pay, this includes your rent or mortgage, household expenses (such as utilities), car insurance payments, estimates for gas and maintenance, credit cards, student loans, and car loans. Add up all of your income and expenses, then subtract your expenses from your income. Here is an example of an "ideal" budget because it covers all expenses and even accounts for savings and investments.

SAMPLE MONTHLY HOUSEHOLD AND PERSONAL BUDGET

Gross Income *		$ 6,670
Expenses:		
Taxes and 401(k)/403(b)		
Federal Withholding	(914)	
Social Security	(413)	
Medicare	(97)	
New York State Tax Withholding	(356)	
SDI	(8)	
401(k)/403(b) Savings	(660)	
Savings/Emergency Fund	(200)	
Rent/Mortgage	(1,600)	
Groceries	(300)	
Utilities (Cable, Electric, Gas)	(200)	
Wireless Telephone	(100)	
Transportation		
Car Note	(300)	
Fuel	(200)	
Car Insurance	(150)	
Maintenance	(50)	

Credit Cards	(300)	
Student Loan	(400)	
Clothing (including purchases and dry cleaning)	(150)	
Entertainment	(150)	
Travel	(120)	
Expenses Subtotal	(6,669)	
		$ (6,669)
		$ 1

*Based on annual gross income of $80,000

The key is to look at your proposed budget and see if it compares to your actual expenditures. Accuracy will be determined by what you say you should have available on your monthly statement vs. what you actually have available in your accounts or on hand.

People have the biggest problem when they do not list all of their expenses or anticipated spending. You may have items of nominal value that you spend but for which you don't account, like that cup of coffee you purchase every day. You might allocate $100 a month for dining out but are actually spending $300. The best way to eliminate this problem would be to literally record your expenditures each day so that you can get an accurate picture of what you're spending. So utilize your smart phone or a small notebook, and for one month or two, write down every single expense and see how that compares to the expenses you have listed on your budget. Then adjust your budget accordingly. Here is an example of Karen's actual budget that reflects her actual expenditures:

KAREN'S MONTHLY HOUSEHOLD AND PERSONAL BUDGET	
Gross Income *	**$ 6,670**
Expenses:	
Taxes and 401(k)/403(b)	
Federal Withholding	(914)
Social Security	(413)
Medicare	(97)
New York State Tax Withholding	(356)
SDI	(8)
401(k)/403(b) Savings	(660)
Savings/Emergency Fund	(200)
Rent/Mortgage	(2,000)
Groceries/Dining out	(500)

Utilities (Cable, Electric, Gas)	(300)	
Wireless Telephone	(200)	
Transportation		
Car Note	(300)	
Fuel	(200)	
Car Insurance	(150)	
Maintenance	(50)	
Credit Cards	(500)	
Student Loan	(400)	
Clothing (including purchases and dry cleaning)	(150)	
Personal Hygiene	(100)	
Entertainment	(150)	
Travel	(120)	
Expenses Subtotal	(7,769)	
		$ (7,769)
		$ (1,099)

Now here's the beauty—finetuning your budget. After you get an accurate assessment or accounting of all your income and all of your expenses, you will see exactly where you stand in terms of savings and investing. If your income is greater than your expenses, that means you have money to save or invest. If your expenses are greater than your income, then you have to find ways to reduce your expenses. Otherwise, you will have no money to save or invest. The other option would be to increase your income to offset your expenses.

For example, when I was tightening the reins on my spending, I decided not to use cable. I literally cut the cord and decided to get an online streaming service as opposed to using a cable provider. I now have only internet service with the cable provider. As a result, I save $50 a month. Now $50 a month may not sound like a lot, but over a year, that's a savings of $600 that can be placed into an account or that can be used towards debt reduction. I pretty much watched only two channels, so I did not need a 500-channel cable package. If you find a couple items that you can cut out, you'd be surprised at how much money you can save. But the key is to be mindful and be truthful on where you spend.

Here are some other tips to reduce your spending:

- Stop eating out so much. Cook at home. It is much healthier and costs less. Bring lunch to work. Let's say you spend $10 for lunch per day. If you decide to bring lunch, you could potentially save nearly $2.5K per year! Here is the math: $10 per day x 5 days per week is $50 per week. Multiply this by 48 weeks in a year, and you get $2.4K! That is significant!

⊙ Stop the 3pm coffee or tea runs, which can save you $40 to $50 dollars each month and over $600 per year! Bring your own coffee or tea to work or school.

⊙ Get rid of cable. Most likely, you watch just a few channels anyway. Switch to an internet streaming provider like Hulu, Netflix, or YouTube and watch content on your computer.

⊙ Shop with a grocery list and stick to it. Never go food shopping when hungry, as you end up buying more items you normally would not buy. Use coupons.

⊙ Call your credit card company and negotiate lower interest rates.

⊙ Reduce utilities such as electricity and gas expenses. Change all your light bulbs to the most efficient types. Only use the lights, air conditioner, and heat as necessary. Upgrade your electrical units at home.

⊙ Reduce impulse shopping. Learn to discern a need from a want. Shop at consignment or thrift shops.

⊙ Leave the credit/charge cards at home and use cash.

Here is Karen's revised budget, which should look familiar because it's the "perfect" budget presented earlier in the chapter.

KAREN'S MONTHLY HOUSEHOLD AND PERSONAL BUDGET	
Gross Income *	**$ 6,670**
Expenses:	
Taxes and 401(k)/403(b)	
Federal Withholding	(914)
Social Security	(413)
Medicare	(97)
New York State Tax Withholding	(356)
SDI	(8)
401(k)/403(b) Savings	(660)
Savings/Emergency Fund	(200)
Rent/Mortgage	(1,600)
Groceries/Dining out	(300)
Utilities (Cable, Electric, Gas)	(200)
Wireless Telephone	(100)
Transportation	
Car Note	(300)

Fuel	(200)
Car Insurance	(150)
Maintenance	(50)
Credit Cards	(200)
Student Loan	(400)
Clothing (including purchases and dry cleaning)	(150)
Personal Hygiene	(100)
Entertainment	(150)
Travel	(120)
Expenses Subtotal	(6,669)
	$ (6,669)
	$ 1

I personally bring my lunch to work. I have stopped window shopping because I would find myself walking into a store and making unnecessary and impulsive purchases. I do not carry large amounts of cash or my credit cards on me. I only carry my debit card. I will only carry my credit card if I'm taking a long trip somewhere. I live in a city, so I only need my MetroCard to get around. Without large amounts of cash or credit card on hand, I'll think twice about the purchase. I am very careful about using my debit card at retail establishments or even online because of online hackers (once they get hold of the debit card information, they can pretty much wipe out your account). I will only use my debit card on very rare occasions. So I'm very diligent about using my debit card outside of my bank's ATM machine. Now that I eat more at home, my meals are much healthier; dining out is now considered a treat as opposed to a way of life. When I plan or contemplate a big-ticket item, I always tie it to a special occasion. For example, when I passed my medical boards, I bought a nice bracelet. When I graduated from medical school, I bought myself a really nice handbag. When I make a large purchase, it is always tied to a particular accomplishment. I feel like at that point, I deserve the purchase, and it's a nice reminder of what I accomplished. I will never walk into a store and just make a random large purchase just because I see it and want it. So be very intentional with how you spend your money. Respect the dollar. Another alternative is instead of treating yourself with a bag or shoes, something that can depreciate in value, buy yourself stock or place money into a special account that you plan to use towards a real estate purchase or something that generates revenue for you.

Now, if you have reduced your expenses as much as you are able to and still find yourself in a deficit, you will have to find ways to increase your income. And there are tons of opportunities for you to do just that. Here are some tips to increase your income.

- Monetize your hobby. If you enjoy cooking, offer your services to cook and serve at a small dinner. If you are an artist, sell your art. If you love dogs, start a dog walking service.

- Write a blog, articles, or a book.

- Sign up for overtime or extra shifts on your job.

- Find a second job.

- Sell unwanted items like clothes or household items. You can hold a garage sale or sell online or sell items to a consignment shop.

- Start a business.

NOTES

NOTES

NOTES

NOTES

NOTES

CHAPTER 6

Protecting Your Assets

*Financial security and independence are
like a three-legged stool resting on savings,
insurance, and investments.*

—Brian Tracy

The next step in personal finance is protecting your assets. It's necessary to protect your assets because things happen in life over which you have no control. You may acquire an illness, have damage to your home or apartment, or get into a car accident. Having insurance helps protect against any unexpected events that might occur. There are various types of insurance, all of which are equally important. Let's break them down one by one.

1. Health Insurance – Protection for your health that can be obtained by either your employer, di-

rectly from insurance, or through the health insurance marketplace. Here are the different types you many consider (www.healthcare.gov):

- Exclusive Provider Organization (EPO): A plan where services are covered only if you use physicians, specialists, or hospitals in the plan's network (except in an emergency).

- Health Maintenance Organization (HMO): An insurance plan that usually limits coverage to care from physicians who work for or contract with the HMO. It normally does not cover out-of-network care except in an emergency.

- Point of Service (POS): A plan where you pay less if you use physicians, hospitals, and other health care providers that belong to the plan's network. You many need referrals from your primary care physician to consult with a specialist.

- Preferred Provider Organization (PPO): A plan where you pay less if you use providers in the plan's network. You can use physicians, hospitals, and other providers outside of the network without a referral for an additional cost.

2. Automobile Insurance – Protection for your automobile. Coverage may include protection for collisions, bodily harm, property damage, and medical payments. It also provides for liability, which would cover you should you injure another person or cause damage to another person's property with your automobile.

3. Home Insurance – Protection for your home and other items like landscaping or a shed. However, the land is not insured. It also protects the contents of your home, like appliances and clothing. You also have liability protection to cover you should a guest become injured on your property or suffer a loss or damage on your property, such as destruction of a car. Renters insurance protects your property within your rental.

4. Life Insurance – Protection that provides benefits for your beneficiaries. There are two main types of policies: term and whole (cash value).

   ▸ Term life policies pay a death benefit to your beneficiaries if you die during the specific term of the policy. Term policy time periods may range from one year to thirty years.

- ❯ Whole life policies provide permanent coverage that lasts a lifetime as well as guaranteed premiums (premiums that do not increase with age) and a guaranteed cash value that the policyholder may borrow against or withdraw depending on the policy terms. Whole life policies are usually more expensive than term life policies.

5. Disability Insurance — Protection that provides income during a non-work related disability that prevents you to work and provides income for yourself. Most insurance policies will replace 60 to 80 percent of your after-tax income.

ESTATE PLANNING

One of the reasons why financial wellness is important and why we want to get a good handle on our finances is because we want to leave a legacy for our loved ones when we are no longer here. Yes, you should enjoy life and spend your hard earnings accordingly and have the funds to do things that you enjoy, but if you have children, siblings, nieces, or nephews about whom you care, you may want to leave them a bulk of your estate. However, in order to do that, you have to make your wishes known legally. One way to do this is estate planning. I will cover the main points, however, you should always consult a lawyer for more detailed planning.

1. According to Northwest Mutual, there are key six key steps to estate planning (https://www.north-westernmutual.com/life-and-money/the-estate-planning-process-6-steps-to-take/):

   - ❯ Create an inventory of what you own and what you owe.

   - ❯ Develop a contingency plan just in case you or your spouse dies.

   - ❯ Provide for children and dependents through beneficiary agreements and through a will.

   - ❯ Protect your assets and document your wishes via will and trust.

   - ❯ Appoint fiduciaries or executors who are responsible for carrying out your wishes.

NOTES

NOTES

NOTES

NOTES

NOTES

CHAPTER 7

Credit Cards

*Make this the year you tackle that credit
card debt once and for all.*

—Suze Orman

What is a credit card and why do we use it? A credit card
is a financial instrument, usually an actual card issued by
a bank, retail establishment, or financial establishment,
allowing you to purchase goods or services on credit.

Credit card usage is one of the most common causes
of financial mismanagement and a leading reason many
live beyond their means. Many people will purchase
items using plastic for either convenience or because
they do not have the cash on hand to buy it outright. Depending on the interest rate of your card tacked on your
balance, you could be paying off an item for many, many,

many years—more years than necessary. For example, you may charge a $500 television. It can take three to four years to pay off that balance if you pay only the minimum payment each time. This can rob you of the ability to save and invest for more important things like retirement. Here are the components of credit cards that you must understand.

COMPONENTS OF CREDIT CARDS
(https://www.wellsfargo.com/help/faqs/credit-card-glossary/)

- **Annual Fee:** A fee that may be charged once a year for maintaining an account and for any special services, depending on the specific terms of your card account.

- **Annual Percentage Rate (APR):** The periodic rate, expressed as an annual amount, used to compute the interest charge on an outstanding balance.

- **Authorization:** The approval by the credit card issuer for a merchant or another affiliate to complete a credit card transaction.

- **Automatic Payment:** A free service that automatically makes credit card payments by transferring funds from your checking or savings account to your credit card account.

◉ **Available Credit:** The amount of unused credit available. Available credit is computed by subtracting the outstanding balance from your total credit line.

◉ **Average Daily Balance:** The average balance for each day in the billing period, calculated by adding all daily balances together and dividing that total amount by the number of days in the billing period.

◉ **Balance:** An outstanding amount of money. A checking or savings account balance refers to the amount of money in a particular account. A credit card balance refers to the amount owed.

◉ **Balance Transfer:** Allows you to use the available credit on one credit card and pay off another, ideally with a lower cost.

◉ **Billing Cycle:** The number of days in the billing period. It includes the day after the previous close date through the current closing date of the account.

◉ **Cardholder Agreement:** The cardholder agreement details the terms and conditions of your credit card account and includes the rate, fees, and other cost information associated with the account.

- **Cash Advance:** A cash advance is an advance of funds from your card account. Cash advances are typically more expensive than other credit card transactions, and fees may also apply to each cash advance taken on an account. Typically, there is no grace period for a cash advance, and interest begins to accrue immediately. You will need to refer to the specific terms of your account to determine the cost of any card transaction, including cash advances.

- **Credit:** Credit is a promise to repay a debt for purchases you make. It allows you to buy something today and pay for it later. Building a good credit history can help you buy a house or even get a job.

- **Credit Bureau:** A credit-reporting agency that checks credit information and keeps files on people who apply for and use credit. The credit bureau produces a credit report, which is a record of a consumer's level of indebtedness and bill-paying behavior. The agencies compile the report and release it to lenders and others as permitted by law.

- **Credit Line:** Also known as credit limit, this is the maximum amount you can carry as the balance on your credit card. If you exceed this amount, an over-the-credit-limit fee may be imposed.

- **Credit Score:** Also known as a credit rating. Many lenders use this numeric calculation of your credit report to obtain a fast, objective measure of your credit risk and consider your score when deciding whether or not to approve a loan.

- **Float:** When a cardholder makes a purchase or obtains an advance, the transactions may not post for a few days. The charge amount is not added to the balance of the account until the transaction does post. The time between purchase and posting is referred to as the float.

- **Grace Period:** The period between the date of the credit card billing statement and the date payment in full must be received before interest begins to accrue on new purchases.

- **Interest:** Interest is the fee for borrowing money. Interest is listed on your credit card statement as "Interest Charge."

- **Interest Rate:** The percent per unit of time that a bank or financial institution charges a customer for borrowing money.

- **Introductory Rates:** Credit cards often offer lower introductory APRs as special promotional offers.

These are typically only given on a limited time basis, and after the introductory period, the rate usually returns to the standard rate on the account. It's important to read the terms and conditions for all credit cards to fully understand how long the introductory rate will last and what the rate will be at the end of the introductory period.

- **Issuer:** An issuer (or issuing member) is a financial institution that issues credit cards, such as Visa® or MasterCard®.

- **Late Payment Fee:** The charge that may be imposed if the minimum monthly payment is not received by the payment due date.

- **Linked Account:** Sometimes a credit card account may be linked to another account so that funds may be transferred electronically between accounts.

- **Minimum Interest:** Please refer to your Customer Agreement and Disclosure Statement for the minimum interest on your specific credit card account.

- **Minimum Monthly Payment:** The minimum dollar amount that must be paid each month to prevent a credit card account from being delinquent. The amount is based on the percentage of your outstanding balance or could be a minimum fixed amount, depending on the terms of the account.

⊙ **Outstanding Balance:** The amount you owe on your credit card. This is the balance used to calculate payments and on which interest is charged.

⊙ **Overdraft Protection:** This is a feature offered on many credit card accounts that allows a customer to link their checking account to their credit card for purposes of covering any overdrafts that may occur on the checking account. Fees and terms may vary from account to account.

⊙ **Over-the-Credit-Limit Fee:** A fee that may be imposed if your outstanding balance exceeds your credit limit.

⊙ **Payment Due Date:** The date when your payment must reach your bank in order to avoid a late payment fee (if applicable).

⊙ **PIN:** Personal Identification Numbers (PINs) are secret numbers that customers use to access their accounts via ATMs.

⊙ **Prime Rate:** Many credit cards use the "prime rate" as a base rate (e.g., "prime + 12 percent"). The prime rate used is taken from the Money Rates column of *The Wall Street Journal*. The prime rate is merely a base rate used to make loans to certain borrowers. It is not necessarily the lowest or best rate at which loans are made. The credit card issuer discloses the manner in which the rate is determined in the Customer Agreement and Disclosure Statement.

- **Purchases:** Credit card charges you make at merchants. Purchases usually have a lower APR than other account transactions such as cash advances.

- **Secured Credit Card:** A credit card that requires you to pledge collateral to receive credit. Often, your credit line is determined by the amount you deposit into a collateral account.

- **Unsecured Credit Card:** A credit card that is not secured with collateral. A customer may qualify for unsecured credit based on their credit history and financial strength.

- **Additional Cards:** Cards issued on an account not in the primary or secondary name. Additional cardholders are authorized to charge to the card and make payments. They can also check the balance and available credit on the account. Additional cardholders are not authorized to make changes to the account. Please remember that you are responsible for all charges made to the card in addition to any balance transfers and cash advances, including any overdraft protection amounts advanced, made by any additional cardholders added to the account.

WHAT IS A CREDIT REPORT?

A credit report details your credit history. It lists everywhere you've lived and worked, all the credit cards or loans you owe, payment information, how many times you've applied for credit, liens, bankruptcy, and judgments. It really gives you a snapshot of where you are in terms of your overall credit life. Creditors look at these credit reports to make decisions based on your credit worthiness. It's imperative to monitor your credit report regularly. It is not only for you to see where you stand, but it will also tell you if there is fraud or if someone opened up an account in your name. There are so many options for obtaining a credit report. I love creditkarma.com and annualcreditreport.com because they are free. The main companies that provide information to the credit reports are credit reporting agencies. These agencies include:

1. Equifax: P.O. Box 740241, Atlanta, GA 30374-0241, 1-800-685-1111.

2. Experian: P.O. Box 2104, Allen, TX 75013-0949, 1-888-EXPERIAN (397-3742)

3. TransUnion: P.O. Box 1000, Chester, PA 19022, 1-800-916-8800.

FICO SCORE – WHAT IS IT AND WHY IS IT IMPORTANT?

Although there are many types of credit scores, the FICO score is the most widely used. The FICO score is a credit score created by the Fair Isaac Corporation. Creditors utilize these scores along with credit reports to determine whether potential borrowers are worthy of credit based on risk. The FICO score takes into account a borrower's payment history, current level of indebtedness, types of credit used, length of credit history, and new credit accounts.

Think of your FICO score as a grade. The top grade, an "A," is equivalent to a FICO score of 850, and an "F" would be a credit score of 350. Most lenders like FICO scores above 650.

FICO scores are extremely important, and I cannot express this enough. Also understand that minute changes in your payment or timeliness in payments can affect your FICO score. For example, a 30-day late payment can drop your credit score by 10 to 20 points or more. If you're late on your mortgage, the drop in your score can be as much as 50 points, and if you file for bankruptcy, your score can drop as much as 100 points. It's much harder to build up your score than it is for it to decrease. If you are 30 days late on payment on one of your cards, it may take between one and six months to see an improvement in your score. Depending on the severity of the lateness and on what has been placed on your credit report, it may take time to recover. If you file for bankruptcy, that information stays on your credit report for as long as 10 years. A late payment stays on for seven years. However, late payments made within a two-year period are more scrutinized than late payments older than two years. It really depends on the lender and how they want to interpret your credit information. In general, if you have a lot of 30-day late payments or a few 60- to 90-day late payments, including charge-offs (where the credit card company decides to write off your balance as a loss because they have decided there is a high probability that they will never recover the credit card balance), this will reflect poorly on your credit report. Think of your FICO score as a representation of everything that is presented on your credit report and a testament to how you pay your bills and how financially responsible you are.

THE BOTTOM LINE

Proper usage of credit cards and loans determine how well you do financially. For example, if you're overextended on a credit card and you're paying the minimum payment on large balances, this will take away from what you can save and invest for the future if you're not mindful. Not paying your bills on time can prevent you from obtaining more credit in the future, especially for large purchases such as a home a car. It can also affect the interest rate that you get. Normally, the better your credit, the more favorable interest rates are given to you on all types of loans. Similarly, the worse off your credit is, the more expensive it is for you to obtain proper credit. Interest rates can range from 0 percent to 26 or 27 percent on various financial products. So although you want to use credit, use it at a minimum and use it responsibly. And yes, credit is a necessity in this day and age because no credit is viewed as bad credit. If you have no credit, there is absolutely nothing the lender can go off of in terms of your credit worthiness. If you have bad credit, then they know that you may not be the most financially worthy person of their product.

NOTES

NOTES

NOTES

NOTES

CHAPTER 8

Saving and Investments

Money looks better in the bank than on your feet.

—Sophia Amoruso

The next step in finances is saving and investing. Depending on your age, savings and investing should start after you pay off your debt. In theory, you get a guaranteed return on your money when you no longer pay interest vs. the interest you may earn on money saved. If you have no debt or have paid it off, it's time for savings. The earlier you start saving and investing, the more you reap. Why? It is due to a concept called compounding interest. According investors.gov, "compound interest" is the interest you earn on interest. This can be illustrated by using basic math: if you have $100 and it earns 5 percent interest each year, you'll have $105 at the end of the first year. At the end of the second year, you'll have

$110.25. Not only did you earn $5 on the initial $100 deposit, you also earned $0.25 on the $5 in interest. While 25 cents may not sound like much at first, it adds up over time. Even if you never add another dime to that account, in 10 years you'll have more than $162 thanks to the power of compound interest, and in 25 years, you'll have almost $340." This is just a small investment. Can you imagine how much can be accumulated with regular investments? Our friend Karen decided to take the $200 allocation from her budget and deposit it into a mutual fund account with an average 6 percent interest rate of return on investment In twenty years, that investment will be worth $88,000! That is a significant amount of money. And it is all due to steady, regular investments over a period of time.

EMERGENCY FUND

Your first savings should be for your emergency fund, which is fund that you set aside for unexpected emergencies, such as a loss of job or income, a medical expense, or temporary disability. Most advisors will say you should have an equivalent of six months' take-home pay in your emergency fund.

SHORT-TERM SAVINGS

Your next savings goal should be for short-term purposes (a period of two years or less). This money should be saved in an investment that is as close to cash as possible. You can save in either a banking savings account or a money market account. You want to keep as much principal as possible. Due to the short-term time period, your savings account cannot and should not absorb the fluctuation that can occur in regular stocks accounts.

LONG-TERM SAVINGS/INVESTING

Long-term savings are savings you accumulate over a period of time longer than two years. In these scenarios, you are most likely saving for retirement, a home, or a car. Most long-term savings can withstand fluctuations in the market. These are savings you will not access frequently, and in the case of retirement, you normally will not touch it until retirement.

Think of the various types of investments as tools that can help you achieve your financial goals. Each broad investment type—from bank products to stocks and bonds—has its own general set of features, risk factors, and ways in which they can be used by investors.

Learn more about the various types of investments below as described by firma.org.

- **Bank Products:** Banks and credit unions can provide a safe and convenient way to accumulate savings—and some banks offer services that can help you manage your money. Checking and savings accounts offer liquidity and flexibility.

- **Bonds:** A bond is a loan an investor makes to an organization in exchange for interest payments over a specified term plus repayment of principal at the bond's maturity date.

- **Stocks:** When you buy shares of a company's stock, you own a piece of that company. Stocks come in a wide variety, and they often are described based the company's size, type, performance during market cycles and potential for short- and long-term growth.

- **Investment Funds:** Funds pool money from many investors and invest it according to a specific investment strategy. Funds can offer diversification, professional management, and a wide variety of investment strategies and styles.

- **Annuities:** An annuity is a contract between you and an insurance company in which the company promises to make periodic payments, either starting immediately—called an immediate annuity—or at some future time—a deferred annuity.

❯ **Retirement:** Numerous types of investments come into play when saving for retirement and managing income once you retire. For saving, tax-advantaged retirement options such as a 401(k) or an IRA can be a smart choice. Managing retirement income may require moving out of certain investments and into ones that are better suited to a retirement lifestyle.

❯ ****Options:** Options are contracts that give the purchaser the right, but not the obligation, to buy or sell a security, such as a stock or exchange-traded fund, at a fixed price within a specific period of time.

❯ ****Commodity Futures:** Commodity futures contracts are agreements to buy or sell a specific quantity of a commodity at a specified price on a particular date in the future. Commodities include metals, oil, grains, and animal products, as well as financial instruments and currencies. With limited exceptions, trading in futures contracts must be executed on the floor of a commodity exchange.

❯ ****Security Futures:** Federal regulations permit trading in futures contracts on single stocks, also known as single stock futures, and certain security indices.

**Options, Commodity, and Security Future funds are not instruments you will purchase as a beginner.

Since you are most likely a beginner, your first investments would most likely involve mutual funds. Mutual funds can be further classified by the following types of funds as described by mutualfunds.com.

❯ **Small-cap funds** invest primarily in stocks in companies worth between $300 million and $2 billion, but the size can vary for each fund. Mutual funds have restrictions that limit them from buying large portions of any one issuer's outstanding shares, which limits the risk while giving an investor exposure to this segment of the market.

❯ **A mid-cap fund** invests in companies worth between $2 billion to $10 billion in market cap, but again, this definition can change depending on the fund. These are established businesses that are still considered developing and thus have a higher growth rate than large-cap funds.

◈ **Large-cap funds** invest in stocks in the largest companies in the world, with market caps in excess of $10 billion. These include Apple, Exxon, and Google. They have a lower growth rate than small-cap funds and mid-cap funds, but they are typically safer, and some provide dividends, giving an extra boost to returns.

◈ **Foreign equity funds, or global/international funds**, invest in a specific region outside of an investor's home country. These funds sometimes have very high returns, but it is hard to classify them as either riskier or safer than domestic investments. There are a number of additional risks that have to be considered, including unique country and political risks. As part of a balanced portfolio, they can add additional returns and are worth considering.

◈ **Fixed income funds (better known as bond funds)** invest in debt issued by local and national governments and large companies.

◈ **Balanced funds (also called hybrid funds)** hold both equity (stock) and fixed income (bond) investments in one fund.

MORE ON RETIREMENT ACCOUNTS

If you are a working adult, you may have given thought to retirement savings. Here is a glossary of at least four types of retirement savings accounts that the average person (non-business owner or business owner with no employees) may consider:

- **401(k) or 403(b)** — For most people, these two plans are the most common. A 401(k) is normally offered to employees of for-profit companies, and a 403(b) is normally offered to employees of nonprofit companies. Contributions are made from your paycheck with pretax dollars (before tax withholdings). In 2018, the maximum amount that can be contributed is $18,500 of your pretax income ($24,500 if you are 50 or older). This money can be rolled over into new 401(k) or a personal IRA account if you leave your job. If you decide to withdraw this money, heavy income tax penalties can occur if you are younger than 59 ½ years old, however, there are some exceptions that you should confirm with your accountant.

- **Solo 401(k)** — A sole proprietor can set up an individual 401(k) and make contributions as both the employee and employer. Per the Internal Revenue Service (IRS), contributions can be made to the plan in both capacities. The maximum that can be contributed in 2018 is $55,000 or $61,000 is you are 50 years or older.

- **Traditional IRA** — Per IRS guidelines, almost anyone can contribute up to $5,500 in 2018 to an IRA ($6,500 if you're over 50) regardless of income. The interest and gains on your IRA are not taxed (tax-deferred) until it is distributed. These contributions may be tax deductible if you qualify, and you can contribute until age 70 ½. If you withdraw prior to age 59 ½, you may incur income tax penalties with some exceptions (check with your accountant). In addition, distributions are required at age 70 1/2. Per the IRS, you are able to contribute to a traditional IRA whether or not you participate in another retirement plan through your employer or business. However, you may not be able to deduct all of your contributions from your income if you or your spouse participates in another retirement plan at work. (Again, confer with your accountant.)

- **Roth IRA** — Per IRS and income guidelines, almost anyone can contribute up to $5,500 in 2018 to a Roth IRA ($6,500 if you're over 50). Unlike a traditional IRA, you cannot deduct your contribution against your gross income during tax preparation time. The money you earn accumulates tax-free, and you pay no tax on withdrawals after you reach age 59 ½ (and if you had your account for at least 5 years). Plus, unlike with regular IRAs, there is no mandatory withdrawal at age 70 ½ (meaning you can also leave amounts in your Roth IRA as long as you live). You can withdraw the amount you contributed (but not your earnings) at any time with no penalty or no taxes due, which is not the case with traditional IRAs. There are income guidelines, therefore consult with your accountant or tax advisor to see whether or not you can contribute to a Roth IRA. You can contribute to both a Roth IRA and a traditional IRA, but the limits apply to your total contribution. Also consult with your accountant regarding Roth IRA withdrawals and penalty rules, because they vary depending on your age.

In any case, saving for retirement is crucial. Please consult with an accountant or tax advisor to discuss the various options and how they affect you from a tax standpoint.

NOTES

NOTES

NOTES

NOTES

CHAPTER 9

Your Financial Team

Great things in business are never done by one person. They're done by a team of people.

—Steve Jobs

To get on the path to financial wellness, you must have a team. I know that sounds fancy, but it's not. The importance of having the right people on your team cannot be understated. You need to find experts who know all the particular aspects of financial planning. No one is an island who can achieve these things by themselves. So here are the main people you should have on your financial team. Your first person should be your financial planner. That person is responsible for managing or directing your personal finance. Now that does not mean you just hand them over all your information and they come up with a decision. You and your financial planner work hand in hand. You provide all of your information along with your goals, and together, you should work towards a very realistic and doable plan.

The next important person is your accountant. This person is responsible for reconciling your records to your accounts. You can actually use a bookkeeper for this as well. Some will say that you don't need an accountant, but at the very least, you should use one during tax preparation time, because an accountant will be responsible for knowing all the latest tax laws and will be able to prepare your tax return in the most complete way.

The next person with whom you may want to establish a relationship is a banker. Your banker is your point person to whom you can speak regarding your checking and savings accounts and investment accounts. If you run into a financial issue, having a relationship with one person at your bank can prove to be very beneficial. Usually it does not cost you anything. What I personally like about having a banker is that they can offer and discuss various banking products, like different checking accounts, savings accounts, and investment accounts that are tailored to your situation.

The most important person on your team is you. You should never leave all your devices, including all your information, to third parties. You should always be educated on anything that affects your finances. I'm sure you've heard stories of people who took a hands-off approach to their finances. They left the decision making to a spouse or significant other or completely to their accountant or investment banker. The next thing you know, that person's finances were completely wiped out. You should understand the basic tenants of checking, savings, and investing and where each one of your dollars are going. There are plenty of online sources and books that you can obtain to increase your financial knowledge. You don't necessarily need to become an expert, but you should have basic understanding so that you can be a collaborator with the financial professionals.

NOTES

NOTES

NOTES

NOTES

NOTES

CHAPTER 10

Resources

It's best to have your tools with you.
If you don't, you're apt to find something you
didn't expect and get discouraged.

—Stephen King

- Yahoo Finance

- Kiplingers

- Mint – www.mint.com

- YNAB – www.youneedabudget.com

- Robinhood (introduction to investing)

- Investopedia's Investing 101 Tutorial

- Motley fools

- Investeopedia

- https://www.paycheckcity.com

- Investors.gov

NOTES

NOTES

NOTES

NOTES

ABOUT THE AUTHOR

As one of the nation's most acclaimed pediatricians and financial wellness experts, Dr. Randi B. Nelson (aka DrRandiBMD) is also a nationally recognized author, speaker, and consultant. In addition, she is a sought-after media expert regarding children's and young adults' health issues. Due to her 14-year career in investment banking, she is also a financial wellness expert.

Dr. Randi is a published author in the *Chicken Soup for the Soul* series with her short autobiographical story *Following My Heart*.

Dr. Randi earned her BS in Accounting from State University of New York, Buffalo, her MBA from Hofstra University, and her MD from State University of New

York, Stony Brook School of Medicine. She completed her pediatric residency at Jacobi Medical Center in the Bronx, New York.

Dr. Randi currently lives in Brooklyn, New York. To connect, email her at DrRandi@DrRandibmd.com

CREATING DISTINCTIVE BOOKS
WITH INTENTIONAL RESULTS

We're a collaborative group of creative masterminds
with a mission to produce high-quality books to position
you for monumental success in the marketplace.

Our professional team of writers, editors, designers,
and marketing strategists work closely together to ensure
that every detail of your book is a clear representation
of the message in your writing.

Want to know more?
Write to us at info@publishyourgift.com
or call (888) 949-6228

Discover great books, exclusive offers, and more at
www.PublishYourGift.com

Connect with us on social media

@publishyourgift